Overleaf: THE EARTHLY PARADISE by Jan Brueghel, the Elder (1568-1625). Member of a great Flemish family of painters founded by Pieter Brueghel, the Elder. The imaginative landscape of the Garden of Eden nearly obscures the figures of Adam and Eve in the background. The painting was completed in 1625, the year of the artist's death.

Detail of the animals from
EARTHLY PARADISE — *Brueghel*

5

Its name was Babel

And they said to one another, "Come, let us make bricks, and burn them thoroughly." And they had brick for stone, and bitumen for mortar.

Then they said, "Come, let us build ourselves a city, and a tower with its top in the heavens, and let us make a name for ourselves, lest we be scattered abroad upon the face of the whole earth."

And the Lord came down to see the city and the tower, which the sons of men had built.

And the Lord said, "Behold, they are one people, and they have all one language; and this is only the beginning of what they will do; and nothing that they propose to do will now be impossible for them.

Come, let us go down, and there confuse their language, that they may not understand one another's speech."

So the Lord scattered them abroad from there over the face of all the earth, and they left off building the city.

Therefore its name was called Babel, because there the Lord confused the language of all the earth; and from there the Lord scattered them abroad over the face of all the earth.

Genesis 11:3-9

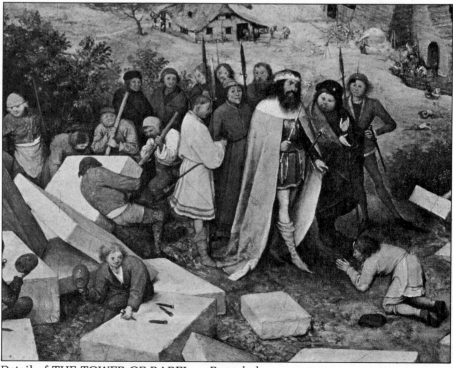

Detail of THE TOWER OF BABEL — *Brueghel*

Overleaf: THE TOWER OF BABEL by Pieter Brueghel, the Elder (1520-1569). Founder of a family of well-known painters, including Pieter the Younger and Jan the Elder. THE TOWER OF BABEL is typical of the imaginative detail with which Brueghel painted his many landscapes.

Overleaf: MOSES SAVED FROM THE WATERS
OF THE NILE by Claudio de Lorena (1600-1632).
Born in the Chamagne Castle in France in 1600,
Lorena belonged to the French School of Painting.

And the child grew

Then Pharaoh commanded all his people, "Every son that is born to the Hebrews you shall cast into the Nile, but you shall let every daughter live."

Now a man from the house of Levi went and took to wife a daughter of Levi.

The woman conceived and bore a son; and when she saw that he was a goodly child, she hid him three months.

And when she could hide him no longer she took for him a basket made of bulrushes, and daubed it with bitumen and pitch; and she put the child in it and placed it among the reeds at the river's brink.

And his sister stood at a distance, to know what would be done to him.

Now the daughter of Pharaoh came down to bathe at the river, and her maidens walked beside the river; she saw the basket among the reeds and sent her maid to fetch it.

When she opened it she saw the child; and lo, the babe was crying. She took pity on him and said, "This is one of the Hebrews' children."

Then his sister said to Pharaoh's daughter, "Shall I go and call you a nurse from the Hebrew women to nurse the child for you?"

And Pharaoh's daughter said to her, "Go." So the girl went and called the child's mother.

And Pharaoh's daughter said to her, "Take this child away, and nurse him for me, and I will give you your wages." So the woman took the child and nursed him.

And the child grew, and she brought him to Pharaoh's daughter, and he became her son; and she named him Moses, for she said, "Because I drew him out of the water."

Exodus 1:22 through 2:10

Detail of MOSES SAVED FROM THE WATERS OF THE NILE — *Lorena*

Overleaf: MOSES AND THE TEN COMMAND-
MENTS by Joseph Maniscalco, contemporary. The
detailed craftsmanship typical of this modern
master of religious art is evident in this rendering of
MOSES AND THE TEN COMMANDMENTS.
Maniscalco is a California artist, well known for his
religious paintings.

And God spoke

"I am the Lord your God, who brought you out of the land of Egypt, out of the house of bondage.

"You shall have no other gods before me.

"You shall not make for yourself a graven image, or any likeness of anything that is in heaven above, or that is in the earth beneath, or that is in the water under the earth;

you shall not bow down to them or serve them; for I the Lord your God am a jealous God, visiting the iniquity of the fathers upon the children to the third and the fourth generation of those who hate me,

but showing steadfast love to thousands of those who love me and keep my commandments.

"You shall not take the name of the Lord your God in vain; for the Lord will not hold him guiltless who takes his name in vain.

"Remember the sabbath day, to keep it holy.

Six days you shall labor, and do all your work;

but the seventh day is a sabbath to the Lord your God; in it you shall not do any work, you, or your son, or your daughter, your manservant, or your maidservant, or your cattle, or the sojourner who is within your gates;

for in six days the Lord made heaven and earth, the sea, and all that is in them, and rested the seventh day; therefore the Lord blessed the sabbath day and hallowed it.

"Honor your father and your mother, that your days may be long in the land which the Lord your God gives you.

"You shall not kill.

"You shall not commit adultery.

"You shall not steal.

"You shall not bear false witness against your neighbor.

"You shall not covet your neighbor's house; you shall not covet your neighbor's wife, or his manservant, or his maidservant, or his ox, or his ass, or anything that is your neighbor's."

Exodus 20:1-17

Again the Lord spoke to Ahaz

Again the Lord spoke to Ahaz,

"Ask a sign of the Lord your God; let it be deep as Sheol or high as heaven."

But Ahaz said, "I will not ask, and I will not put the Lord to the test."

And he said, "Hear then, O house of David! Is it too little for you to weary men, that you weary my God also?

Therefore the Lord himself will give you a sign. Behold, a young woman shall conceive and bear a son, and shall call his name Immanuel.

He shall eat curds and honey when he knows how to refuse the evil and choose the good.

For before the child knows how to refuse the evil and choose the good, the land before whose two kings you are in dread will be deserted.

The Lord will bring upon you and upon your people and upon your father's house such days as have not come since the day that Ephraim departed from Judah — the king of Assyria."

Isaiah 7:10-17

Overleaf: THE ANNUNCIATION by Andrea della Robbia (1436-1525). This famous terra-cotta sculptor was once the director of a Flemish workshop for the production of Della Robbia ware. Andrea was the nephew of Luca della Robbia, who founded the Della Robbia process for glazing sculpture.

Now the birth of Jesus Christ took place in this way. When his mother Mary had been betrothed to Joseph, before they came together she was found to be with child of the Holy Spirit;

and her husband Joseph, being a just man and unwilling to put her to shame, resolved to divorce her quietly.

But as he considered this, behold, an angel of the Lord appeared to him in a dream, saying, "Joseph, son of David, do not fear to take Mary your wife, for that which is conceived in her is of the Holy Spirit;

she will bear a son, and you shall call his name Jesus, for he will save his people from their sins."

All this took place to fulfil what the Lord had spoken by the prophet:

"Behold, a virgin shall conceive and bear a son, and his name shall be called Emmanuel" (which means, God with us).

When Joseph woke from sleep, he did as the angel of the Lord commanded him; he took his wife,

but knew her not until she had borne a son; and he called his name Jesus.

St. Matthew 1:18-25

And he called his name Jesus

Do not be afraid

In the sixth month the angel Gabriel was sent from God to a city of Galilee named Nazareth,

to a virgin betrothed to a man whose name was Joseph, of the house of David; and the virgin's name was Mary.

And he came to her and said, "Hail, O favored one, the Lord is with you!"

But she was greatly troubled at the saying, and considered in her mind what sort of greeting this might be.

And the angel said to her, "Do not be afraid, Mary, for you have found favor with God.

And behold, you will conceive in your womb and bear a son, and you shall call his name Jesus."

St. Luke 1:26-31

Overleaf: IMMACULATE CONCEPTION by Giovanni B. Tiepolo (1696-1770). An Italian painter most famous for his Cleopatra frescoes in the Palazzo Labia, Venice. Completed in 1745, the frescoes brought Tiepolo international recognition. IMMACULATE CONCEPTION is a dramatic example of his decorative style of oil painting.

Courtesy of the Busch-Reisinger Museum, Harvard University

In those days

In those days Mary arose and went with haste into the hill country, to a city of Judah,

and she entered the house of Zechariah and greeted Elizabeth.

And when Elizabeth heard the greeting of Mary, the babe leaped in her womb; and Elizabeth was filled with the Holy Spirit

and she exclaimed with a loud cry, "Blessed are you among women, and blessed is the fruit of your womb!"

St. Luke 1:39-42

TIDINGS OF GREAT JOY — *Plockhorst*

Tidings of Great Joy

And in that region there were shepherds out in the field, keeping watch over their flock by night.

And an angel of the Lord appeared to them, and the glory of the Lord shone around them, and they were filled with fear.

And the angel said to them, "Be not afraid; for behold, I bring you good news of a great joy which will come to all the people;

for to you is born this day in the city of David a Savior, who is Christ the Lord.

And this will be a sign for you: you will find a babe wrapped in swaddling cloths and lying in a manger."

And suddenly there was with the angel a multitude of the heavenly host praising God and saying,

"Glory to God in the highest, and on earth peace among men with whom he is pleased!"

St. Luke 2:8-14

And Mary said,
"My soul magnifies the Lord,
and my spirit rejoices in God
my Savior."

St. Luke 1:46-47

MADONNA AND CHILD — *Lang*

Overleaf: ADORATION OF THE SHEPHERDS by Jacopo Bassano (1510-1592). Bassano spent his early years under the influence of his artist-father, Francesco da Ponte. He later became a student of Titian. While his subjects were largely villages, landscapes, and peasants, Bassano is also well known for his portraits and religious paintings.

Let us go to Bethlehem

When the angels went away from them into heaven, the shepherds said to one another, "Let us go over to Bethlehem and see this thing that has happened, which the Lord has made known to us."

And they went with haste, and found Mary and Joseph, and the babe lying in a manger.

St. Luke 2:15-16

ARRIVAL OF THE SHEPHERDS — *Lerolle*

And when they saw it they made known the saying which had been told them concerning this child;

and all who heard it wondered at what the shepherds told them.

St. Luke 2:17-18

Lo, the star

Now when Jesus was born in Bethlehem of Judea in the days of Herod the king, behold, wise men from the East came to Jerusalem, saying,

"Where is he who has been born king of the Jews? For we have seen his star in the East, and have come to worship him."

When they had heard the king they went their way; and lo, the star which they had seen in the East went before them, till it came to rest over the place where the child was.

When they saw the star, they rejoiced exceedingly with great joy;

and going into the house they saw the child with Mary his mother, and they fell down and worshiped him. Then, opening their treasures, they offered him gifts, gold and frankincense and myrrh.

St. Matthew 2:1-2 and 9-11

Page Opposite: FLIGHT INTO EGYPT — *Murillo*

Overleaf: JOURNEY OF THE MAGI by Sassetta
(Stefano di Giovanni, 1395-1450). This Italian
painter gained his first wide-spread recognition
when he completed a polyptych in 1426. JOURNEY
OF THE MAGI is a beautiful example of Sienese art
with its rich blues and oriental decoration.

Detail of THE REST ON THE FLIGHT INTO EGYPT — David

Now when they had departed, behold, an angel of the Lord appeared to Joseph in a dream and said, "Rise, take the child and his mother, and flee to Egypt, and remain there till I tell you; for Herod is about to search for the child, to destroy him."

And he rose and took the child and his mother by night, and departed to Egypt,

and remained there until the death of Herod. This was to fulfil what the Lord had spoken by the prophet, "Out of Egypt have I called my son."

St. Matthew 2:13-15

Overleaf: THE REST ON THE FLIGHT INTO EGYPT by Gerard David (1460-1523). A Flemish painter schooled in the tradition of the Van Eycks, David was a conservative man who borrowed freely from his predecessors. The delicate touch of reverence so evident in this painting is one characteristic that makes David's paintings so masterful.

VIRGIN OF THE GRAPE — *Mignard*

Is not his mother called Mary?

Is this not
the carpenter's son?

THE SON OF A CARPENTER — *Lafon*

He healed them

And Jesus said to them, "A prophet is not without honor, except in his own country, and among his own kin, and in his own house."

And he could do no mighty work there, except that he laid his hands upon a few sick people and healed them.

And he marveled because of their unbelief. And he went about among the villages teaching.

St. Mark 6:4-6

Overleaf: THE BOY CHRIST by Heinrich Hofmann (1824-1902). This German historical painter is most widely known for his depiction of Christ's life through art. The wisdom and compassion of the youthful Christ, captured so eloquently in this painting, is typical of the depth of feeling Hofmann brought to all his paintings of religious art.

The Beatitudes

Blessed are the poor in spirit, for theirs is the kingdom of heaven.

Blessed are those who mourn, for they shall be comforted.

Blessed are the meek, for they shall inherit the earth.

Blessed are those who hunger and thirst for righteousness, for they shall be satisfied.

Blessed are the merciful, for they shall obtain mercy.

Blessed are the pure in heart, for they shall see God.

Blessed are the peacemakers, for they shall be called sons of God.

Blessed are those who are persecuted for righteousness' sake, for theirs is the kingdom of heaven.

Blessed are you when men revile you and persecute you and utter all kinds of evil against you falsely on my account . . . for your reward is great in heaven.

St. Matthew 5:3-12

The Lord sees not as man sees; man looks on the outward appearance, but the Lord looks on the heart.

I Samuel 16:7

I believe that I shall see the goodness of the Lord in the land of the living.

Psalms 27:13

And the effect of righteousness will be peace, and the result of righteousness, quietness and trust for ever.

Isaiah 32:17

The spirit of man is the lamp of the Lord.

Proverbs 20:27

We look not to the things that are seen but to the things that are unseen; for the things that are seen are transient, but the things that are unseen are eternal.

II Corinthians 4:18

Ask, and it will be given you; seek, and you will find; knock, and it will be opened to you.

St. Matthew 7:7

The Lord searches all hearts, and understands every plan and thought.

I Chronicles 28:9

Godliness is of value in every way, as it holds promise for the present life and also for the life to come.

I Timothy 4:8

He was in the beginning with God; all things were made through him, and without him was not anything made that was made.

John 1:2-3

Overleaf: JESUS DISPUTING WITH THE DOCTORS by Paolo Veronese (1528-1588). Along with Tintoretto, Veronese, an Italian painter, is regarded as one of Italy's greatest decorative painters. He is most noted for his lavish style and unique handling of illusionism.

In the temple

And when he was twelve years old, they went up according to custom;

and when the feast was ended, as they were returning, the boy Jesus stayed behind in Jerusalem. His parents did not know it,

but supposing him to be in the company they went a day's journey, and they sought him among their kinsfolk and acquaintances;

and when they did not find him, they returned to Jerusalem, seeking him.

After three days they found him in the temple, sitting among the teachers, listening to them and asking them questions;

and all who heard him were amazed at his understanding and his answers.

St. Luke 2:42-47

Detail of JESUS DISPUTING WITH THE DOCTORS — *Veronese*

John answered them, "I baptize with water; but among you stands one who you do not know,

even he who comes after me, the thong of whose sandal I am not worthy to untie."

This took place in Bethany beyond the Jordan, where John was baptizing.

The next day he saw Jesus coming toward him, and said,

Behold, the Lamb of God

who takes away the sin of the world!

This is he of whom I said, 'After me comes a man who ranks before me, for he was before me.'

I myself did not know him; but for this I came baptizing with water, that he might be revealed to Israel.

And John bore witness, "I saw the Spirit descend as a dove from heaven, and it remained on him.

I myself did not know him; but he who sent me to baptize with water said to me, 'He on whom you see the Spirit descend and remain, this is he who baptizes with the Holy Spirit.'"

St. John 1:26-33

Painting Opposite: THE GOOD SHEPHERD by Dobson.

Let down the nets

And Simon answered, "Master, we toiled all night and took nothing! But at your word I will let down the nets."

And when they had done this, they enclosed a great shoal of fish; and as their nets were breaking,

they beckoned to their partners in the other boat to come and help them. And they came and filled both the boats, so that they began to sink.

But when Simon Peter saw it, he fell down at Jesus' knees, saying, "Depart from me, for I am a sinful man, O Lord."

For he was astonished, and all that were with him, at the catch of fish which they had taken;

and so also were James and John, sons of Zebedee, who were partners with Simon. And Jesus said to Simon, "Do not be afraid; henceforth you will be catching men."

And when they had brought their boats to land, they left everything and followed him.

St. Luke 5:5-11

"Let the children come to me"

And they were bringing children to him, that he might touch them; and the disciples rebuked them.

But when Jesus saw it he was indignant, and said to them, "Let the children come to me, do not hinder them; for to such belongs the kingdom of God.

Truly, I say to you, whoever does not receive the kingdom of God like a child shall not enter it."

And he took them in his arms and blessed them, laying his hands upon them.

And Jesus looked around and said to his disciples, "How hard it will be for those who have riches to enter the kingdom of God!"

And the disciples were amazed at his words. But Jesus said to them again, "Children, how hard it is to enter the kingdom of God!

It is easier for a camel to go through the eye of a needle than for a rich man to enter the kingdom of God."

And they were exceedingly astonished, and said to him, "Then who can be saved?"

Jesus looked at them and said, "With men it is impossible, but not with God; for all things are possible with God."

St. Mark 10:13-16 and 23-27

Painting Opposite: JESUS AND THE CHILDREN by Hugo Vogel (1855-1920). A German historical genre and portrait painter, Vogel was a pupil of Wilhelm Sohn at Dusseldorf and later won a Gold Medal in Berlin.

"Father, I have sinned"

And he arose and came to his father. But while he was yet at a distance, his father saw him and had compassion, and ran and embraced him and kissed him.

And the son said to him, "Father, I have sinned against heaven and before you; I am no longer worthy to be called your son."

But the father said to his servants, "Bring quickly the best robe, and put it on him; and put a ring on his hand, and shoes on his feet;

and bring the fatted calf and kill it, and let us eat and make merry;

for this my son was dead, and is alive again; he was lost, and is found." And they began to make merry.

St. Luke 15:20-24

Color Reproduction: THE PRODIGAL SON by Leandro Bassano (1557-1634). This Italian painter was a member of the famous Bassano family of artists. He followed the tradition of his father, Jacopo, and has paintings in Dresden, Dublin, Venice and Munich.

"I desire mercy... not sacrifice"

At that time Jesus went through the grainfields on the sabbath; his disciples were hungry, and they began to pluck ears of grain and to eat.

But when the Pharisees saw it, they said to him, "Look, your disciples are doing what is not lawful to do on the sabbath."

He said to them, "Have you not read what David did, when he was hungry, and those who were with him:

how he entered the house of God and ate the bread of the Presence, which it was not lawful for him to eat nor for those who were with him, but only for the priests?

Or have you not read in the law how on the sabbath the priests in the temple profane the sabbath, and are guiltless?

I tell you, something greater than the temple is here.

And if you had known what this means, 'I desire mercy, and not sacrifice,' you would not have condemned the guiltless.

For the Son of man is lord of the sabbath."

St. Matthew 12:1-8

Painting Opposite: CHRIST AND THE PHARISEES
IN THE GRAINFIELD by Rumpel.

Hosanna

And when they drew near to Jerusalem, to Bethphage and Bethany, at the Mount of Olives, he sent two of his disciples,

and said to them, "Go into the village opposite you, and immediately as you enter it you will find a colt tied, on which no one has ever sat; untie it and bring it.

If any one says to you, 'Why are you doing this?' say, 'The Lord has need of it and will send it back here immediately.'"

And they went away, and found a colt tied at the door out in the open street; and they untied it.

And those who stood there said to them, "What are you doing, untying the colt?"

And they told them what Jesus had said; and they let them go.

And they brought the colt to Jesus, and threw their garments on it; and he sat upon it.

And many spread their garments on the road, and others spread leafy branches which they had cut from the fields.

And those who went before and those who followed cried out, "Hosanna! Blessed is he who comes in the name of the Lord!

Blessed is the kingdom of our father David that is coming! Hosanna in the highest!"

St. Mark 11:1-10

Painting Opposite: CHRIST'S ENTRANCE INTO JERUSALEM by Eduard Gebhardt (1838-1925). A lesser-known master of the 19th and 20th centuries, Gebhardt was nonetheless sought after to interpret the scriptures in religious art. This painting is a fine example of the detail in Gebhardt's artwork.

And the cock crowed

And they led Jesus to the high priest; and all the chief priests and the elders and the scribes were assembled.

And Peter had followed him at a distance, right into the courtyard of the high priest; and he was sitting with the guards, and warming himself at the fire.

And as Peter was below in the courtyard, one of the maids of the high priest came;

and seeing Peter warming himself, she looked at him, and said, "You also were with the Nazarene, Jesus."

But he denied it, saying, "I neither know nor understand what you mean." And he went out into the gateway.

And the maid saw him, and began again to say to the bystanders, "This man is one of them."

But again he denied it. And after a little while again the bystanders said to Peter, "Certainly you are one of them; for you are a Galilean."

But he began to invoke a curse on himself and to swear, "I do not know this man of whom you speak."

And immediately the cock crowed a second time. And Peter remembered how Jesus had said to him, "Before the cock crows twice, you will deny me three times." And he broke down and wept.

St. Mark 14:53,54 and 66-72

Painting Opposite: PETER'S REPENTANCE by Ary Scheffer (1795-1858). A Dutch-born painter, Scheffer tried many schools of painting before he finally settled into a style that is basically classicist, as represented by PETER'S REPENTANCE. The painting now hangs in the Metropolitan Museum of Art in New York City.

"Hail, King of the Jews"

And the soldiers led him away inside the palace (that is, the praetorium); and they called together the whole battalion.

And they clothed him in a purple cloak, and plaiting a crown of thorns they put it on him.

And they began to salute him, "Hail, King of the Jews!"

And they struck his head with a reed, and spat upon him, and they knelt down in homage to him.

And when they had mocked him, they stripped him of the purple cloak, and put his own clothes on him. And they led him out to crucify him.

St. Mark 15:16-20

CROWNING WITH THORNS — *Titian*

65

"Ecce Homo"

So Jesus came out, wearing the crown of thorns and the purple robe. Pilate said to them, "Here is the man!"

When the chief priests and the officers saw him, they cried out, "Crucify him, crucify him." Pilate said to them, "Take him yourselves and crucify him, for I find no crime in him."

St. John 19:5-6

They led him away

And as they led him away, they seized one Simon of Cyrene, who was coming in from the country, and laid on him the cross, to carry it behind Jesus.

And there followed him a great multitude of the people, and of women who bewailed and lamented him.

St. Luke 23:26-27

Overleaf: ECCE HOMO by Antonio Ciseri (1821-1891). Ciseri studied at the Academy of Florence and is known for his portraits and dramatic historical paintings. ECCE HOMO is considered to be his masterpiece. It is representative of his elaborate, colorful style.

JOURNEY TO CALVARY — *Tintoretto*

Truly...the son of God

And it was the third hour, when they crucified him.

And the inscription of the charge against him read, "The King of the Jews."

And with him they crucified two robbers, one on his right and one on his left.

And those who passed by derided him, wagging their heads, and saying, "Aha! You who would destroy the temple and build it in three days,

save yourself, and come down from the cross!"

And when the sixth hour had come, there was darkness over the whole land until the ninth hour.

And at the ninth hour Jesus cried with a loud voice, "Eloi, Eloi, lama sabachthani?" which means "My God, my God, why hast thou forsaken me?"

And some of the bystanders hearing it said, "Behold, he is calling Elijah."

And one ran and, filling a sponge full of vinegar, put it on a reed and gave it to him to drink, saying, "Wait, let us see whether Elijah will come to take him down."

And Jesus uttered a loud cry, and breathed his last.

And the curtain of the temple was torn in two, from top to bottom.

And when the centurion, who stood facing him, saw that he thus breathed his last, he said, "Truly this man was the Son of God!"

St. Mark 15:25-30 and 33-39

Overleaf: CHRIST ON THE CROSS by Marten DeVos, the Elder (1532-1603). A Flemish painter who studied first under his father, Pieter, and later under the famous Tintoretto. CHRIST ON THE CROSS is considered one of DeVos' true masterpieces.

Overleaf: WAY TO EMMAUS by Robert Zund
(1827-1909).

Emmaus

That very day two of them were going to a village named Emmaus, about seven miles from Jerusalem,

and talking with each other about all these things that had happened.

While they were talking and discussing together, Jesus himself drew near and went with them.

But their eyes were kept from recognizing him.

And he said to them, "What is this conversation which you are holding with each other as you walk?" And they stood still, looking sad.

Then one of them, name Cleopas, answered him, "Are you the only visitor to Jerusalem who does not know the things that have happened there in these days?"

And he said to them, "What things?" And they said to him, "Concerning Jesus of Nazareth, who was a prophet mighty in deed and word before God and all the people,

and how our chief priests and rulers delivered him up to be condemned to death, and crucified him."

And he said to them, "O foolish men, and slow of heart to believe all that the prophets have spoken!

Was it not necessary that the Christ should suffer these things and enter into his glory?"

St. Luke 24:13-20; 25-26

So when they had come together, they asked him, "Lord, will you at this time restore the kingdom to Israel?"

He said to them, "It is not for you to know times or seasons which the Father has fixed by his own authority.

But you shall receive power when the Holy Spirit has come upon you; and you shall be my witnesses in Jerusalem and in all Judea and Samaria and to the end of the earth."

Acts 1:6-8

Detail of WAY TO EMMAUS — *Zund*

Overleaf: THE ASCENSION by Rembrandt
(1606-1669). Rembrandt, one of the most famous
Dutch painters, illustrated biblical subjects during
his entire life. THE ASCENSION is representative of
the unique interpretation that Rembrandt brings to
all his religious subjects.

Behold

And when he had said this, as they were looking on, he was lifted up, and a cloud took him out of their sight.

And while they were gazing into heaven as he went, behold, two men stood by them in white robes,

and said, "Men of Galilee, why do you stand looking into heaven? This Jesus, who was taken up from you into heaven, will come in the same way as you saw him go into heaven."

Acts 1:9-11

Index of Color Reproductions

editor
Maryjane Hooper Tonn

•

managing editor
Lorraine Obst

•

art editor
Ralph Luedtke

*Biblical selections from
Revised Standard Version*